JAMES WHITBOURN

THE CHORAL COLLECTION

FOR SATB CHOIR

CHESTER MUSIC

Published by

Chester Music
part of The Music Sales Group
14–15 Berners Street, London W1T 3LJ, UK.

Exclusive Distributors:
Music Sales Limited
Distribution Centre, Newmarket Road,
Bury St Edmunds, Suffolk IP33 3YB, UK.

Music Sales Corporation
257 Park Avenue South, New York,
NY 10016, USA.

Music Sales Pty Limited
Level 4, Lisgar House,
30–32 Carrington Street,
Sydney, NSW 2000 Australia.

Order No. CH83578
ISBN 978-1-78305-956-0
This book © Copyright 2015 Chester Music Limited.
All Rights Reserved.

Edited by Jonathan Wikeley.

Printed in the EU.

www.musicsalesclassical.com

Contents

J ames Whitbourn's compositions are admired for their ability to 'expand the experience of classical music beyond the edges of the traditional map of classical styles' (Tom Manoff, *NPR*), *The Observer* describing him as 'a truly original communicator in modern British choral music.'

His largest composition to date is the choral work *Annelies*, which sets words from *The Diary of Anne Frank*. This concert-length work exists in two scorings, one with orchestra and one with chamber ensemble. Other notable works include *Luminosity*, written for Westminster Choir College with the Archedream dance ensemble, *Son of God Mass* and *Requiem canticorum* – both for soprano saxophone, choir and organ – and *The Seven Heavens*, a large-scale work for choir and orchestra portraying the life of C. S. Lewis in the imagery of the seven medieval planets. His works list also features a number of liturgical pieces, including *The Wounds*, a Lenten meditation with words by Michael Symmons Roberts for choir, reader, violin, cello and organ. There are two settings of the Magnificat and Nunc dimittis (written for King's College, Cambridge, and York Minster) and several anthems, including *Among the angels* which was composed for the enthronement of the Bishop of Salisbury.

His choral works have been presented on acclaimed recordings, including several complete discs of his choral music recorded by the Choir of Clare College, Cambridge, the Oxford-based choir Commotio and Williamson Voices of Westminster Choir College. The second recording with Williamson Voices – *Annelies* (Naxos) – earned a Grammy nomination (Best Choral Performance, 56th Grammy Awards, 2013). He has garnered two other Grammy nominations from previous recordings and many other awards as composer, conductor and producer.

James Whitbourn studied at Magdalen College, Oxford. In 2012, he returned to Oxford as an Honorary Research Fellow of St Stephen's House, one of Oxford University's six Permanent Private Halls. With James Jordan, he also co-directs the Westminster Choir College Choral Institute at Oxford which is hosted at St Stephen's House.

Notes by the composer on works in this collection

This is a collection of early twenty-first century music, all the works contained within it having being written between 2002 and 2014. These short pieces for choir and organ reflect some of my collaborative relationships during that period and beyond. Most of the pieces were always intended as free-standing anthems, motets or carols; a few are taken from longer works. Much important commissioning information, and details of the premieres, is given above the titles in the printed scores. I have therefore not duplicated this information in these notes.

A Prayer of Desmond Tutu

The first two works in this collection both belong in South Africa and draw on my own travels to Cape Town. On one visit to this beautiful city, my South African friend took a detour down a winding road and told me we would call in to see whether a friend of his was at home. His friend, it transpired, was Archbishop Desmond Tutu. He was indeed at home that day and appeared at the door in his track suit to welcome us with an unforgettable smile. Not long afterwards, I was asked to set a prayer of his to music. The piece was to include a spoken sounding of the prayer to be delivered by Archbishop Desmond himself. I later made an additional scoring for upper voices and organ, arranged for the boys of Westminster Abbey.

A Prayer from South Africa

Sometime after my project with Desmond Tutu, I was asked to set another South African prayer, one by Alan Paton, the South African anti-apartheid activist and writer. The music I wrote recalls some of the stylistic features I remember hearing in Africa, although the piece itself was written for an English cathedral choir. The request came from Chris Chivers who had previously been a Canon at St George's Cathedral Cape Town and had been in Cape Town at the time of my first visits there.

A Christmas Gloria

A Christmas Gloria is one of the movements of *Missa carolae*, a Christmas Mass scored for piccolo, choir, organ and optional (but highly recommended) brass and percussion. It is based on carol melodies and was written for Midnight Mass on the 1400th anniversary of the founding of Rochester Cathedral. In addition to the opening chords of Praetorius's *Es ist ein Ros' entsprungen* (the music also heard in *A great and mighty wonder*), the movement is based on *God rest ye merry, gentlemen*, though in a rhythmic version which might have been closer to its origins as a dance tune than the more staid version we think of today.

A great and mighty wonder

This is an arrangement of an old German tune for the Christmas carol *Es ist ein Ros' entsprungen*, harmonised by Michael Praetorius (1571–1621). The text comes from a seventh-century Greek poem, *Μέγα καί παράδοξον Θαΰμα*, by St Germanus (634–734), translated in the nineteenth century by John Mason Neale (1818–1866). Neale was heavily influenced by the Oxford Movement led by John Henry Newman (see below) and interested in the rediscovery of ancient sources. Later, Neale's translation was adapted slightly to fit with the tune *Es ist ein Ros' entsprungen*. My arrangement was written for the Choir of King's College, Cambridge.

A Prayer of Cardinal Newman

John Henry Newman was vicar of the University Church in Oxford and was a prime leader in the Oxford Movement, the nineteenth-century movement in the Anglican Church that rediscovered the legacy of the Catholic Church. Newman eventually left the Church of England to be received into the Roman Catholic Church where he was elevated to the rank of cardinal. My setting of his prayer was made at the conclusion of a short residency at Princeton University.

Eternal rest

My longstanding collaboration with the BBC has been the springboard for several pieces within this collection. *Eternal rest* and *Give us the wings of faith* were both written specially for television broadcasts. *Eternal rest* was originally commissioned as an orchestral work and in that form was played for the broadcast of the funeral of Queen Elizabeth the Queen Mother in 2002. In the subsequent choral version, I used text from the Requiem Mass. Because of its original purpose, the opening music quotes a well-known melody by Thomas Arne. There is also a Handelian reference to conjure memories of her coronation as Queen Consort, Empress of India.

Give us the wings of faith

Give us the wings of faith was commissioned for a television programme to celebrate the work of the prolific hymn writer Isaac Watts (Watts' original begins 'Give *me* the wings of faith' but the words are more commonly used in this plural version). The piece also exists in choral and orchestral forms, but this time the choral version is the original with instrumental versions following later (there is also a version for string quartet).

Nunc dimittis

Beside *A great and mighty wonder*, two other pieces in this collection stem from my long association with the Choir of King's College, Cambridge, for whom *Nunc dimittis* and my arrangement of *Were you there?* were composed. *Nunc dimittis* comes from the set of Evening Canticles (*Collegium regale*) written for the choir to perform on Easter Day 2005. The full setting includes a part for (optional) tam-tam which brings extra power to the festal occasion, resoundingly so in the acoustic of King's College Chapel. The tenor solo (first performed by Robert Tear) can be a soloist from within even a small choir since the choral tenor part is never divided.

Pure river of water of life

Two pieces have their genesis in the work of American High School choirs: *Pure river of water of life* and *Video caelos apertos* were both written in response to approaches from directors of music for new works. Both works set texts from the Book of Revelation. *Pure river of water of life* was first performed at Trinity Cathedral, Trenton, NJ under the direction of guest conductor Charles Bruffy. Later, I composed a companion piece for the Oxford choir Commotio: *He carried me away in the spirit*. The two pieces can be performed in an unbroken sequence with the newer work preceding *Pure river of water of life*.

Lux aeterna

Like *Eternal rest* and *Give us the wings of faith*, *Lux aeterna* from *Requiem canticorum* also has its roots in a BBC project, its melody having been composed for a much larger work, *Pika*, commissioned to mark the dropping of the first atomic bomb on the city of Hiroshima. I re-visited the melody in *Requiem canticorum* to give an extra layer of meaning to those who know of that association. The other movements of *Requiem canticorum* all include a part for soprano saxophone and also make use of other works of mine. *Requiem canticorum* was written for the Westminster Williamson Voices and their conductor James Jordan and was premiered in the Alice Tully Hall, New York, with Jeremy Powell the saxophonist.

The Magi's Dream

The two new Christmas carols in this collection, *The Magi's Dream* and *Winter's Wait*, are both settings of words written for me by Robert Tear. Although better known as a singer, Robert Tear was also an artist and writer, and he captures beautifully in both these poems the mixture of naïvety and sophistication that is so often found in medieval carol texts. His words, being written by an expert vocalist, were always fun and rewarding to set to music, and his inventive language offers possibilities for descriptive effects.

There is no speech or language

There is no speech or language comes from my longest choral work, *Annelies*. Almost all of the longer work is a setting of words from the *Diary of Anne Frank*. There are a few small sections, however, that come from other sources, and this is one of them. The words, from the Psalms and from the Book of Lamentations, were chosen for their timeless quality and for the way they relate to so many tragic events in human history. This movement was first performed before the premiere of the full work in a national concert in Westminster Hall within the Houses of Parliament.

Video caelos apertos

Video caelos apertos was written in response to the Church of St John the Evangelist within St Stephen's House, Oxford, to mark a visit by the singers of Medina High School, Ohio as part of their tour to England. The church is an outstanding example of the architecture of the Oxford Movement (see note to *A Prayer of Cardinal Newman*). Its texts combine words reflecting the double dedication, bringing together the martyrdom of Stephen (Acts) with words from the Book of Revelation. The short opening section takes a monophonic form with vocal enhancements that play out the reverberation of a medieval building. After the opening words comes a vision of heaven which depicts the twenty-four elders worshipping night and day.

Were you there?

My setting of this spiritual differs from some other versions in that it includes a resurrection verse, moving as it does from Good Friday to Easter Day. Many other versions set only the verses that cover the events of Good Friday. Naturally, the inclusion of the Easter verse leads to a very different musical treatment with a climactic sequence in the final verse. This arrangement was made for the Choir of King's College, Cambridge, and their conductor Stephen Cleobury.

Winter's Wait

Like *The Magi's Dream*, *Winter's Wait* is a text by my late friend Robert Tear. It shares its tonality with Peter Abelard's beautiful hymn *O quanta qualia* (and also with *Noël nouvelet*) but it bursts into the major for the final stanza. It was first performed by the Choir of King's College, Cambridge, where Robert Tear was an honorary fellow.

James Whitbourn
Oxford
2015

Suggestions for seasonal use

Christmas/Epiphany

A Christmas Gloria

A great and mighty wonder

The Magi's Dream

Winter's Wait

Candlemas

Nunc dimittis

(The Canticle of Simeon)

Lent

There is no speech or language

Were you there?

Easter

Were you there?

Remembrance

A Prayer of Cardinal Newman

Eternal rest

Nunc dimittis

Lux aeterna

Saints' Days

A Prayer of Cardinal Newman

Eternal rest

Give us the wings of faith

Video caelos apertos

General

A Prayer from South Africa

A Prayer of Desmond Tutu

A Prayer of Cardinal Newman

Pure river of water of life

Lux aeterna

Video caelos apertos

Recordings

Recordings of several of the pieces in this collection are available.

Winter's Wait (10); *Give us the wings of faith* (11); *A Prayer from South Africa* (13); *Lux aeterna* (19)

Naxos 8.572737.
James Whitbourn 'Living Voices' (Ken Cowan organ, Westminster Williamson Voices, James Jordan conductor)

Nunc dimittis (2); *A Prayer of Desmond Tutu* (4); *Pure river of water of life* (6); *Eternal rest* (7); *There is no speech or language* (9)

Naxos 8.572103.
James Whitbourn 'Luminosity' (Henry Parkes organ, Commotio, Matthew Berry conductor)

for the choristers of Westminster Abbey, Commonwealth Day 2004

A Prayer of Desmond Tutu

Archbishop Desmond Tutu
(b. 1931)

James Whitbourn
(b.1963)

* *Choir chords to follow the pace of the spoken prayer, which should flow smoothly and without pauses. Exact coincidence of speech and music is not required.*

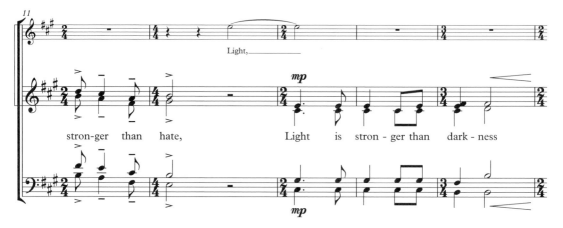

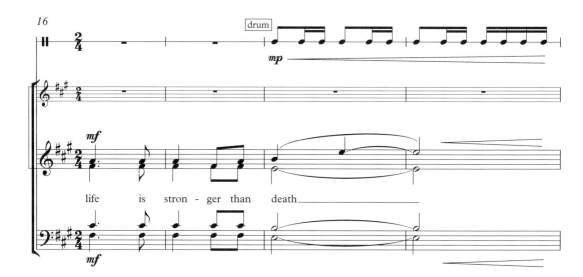

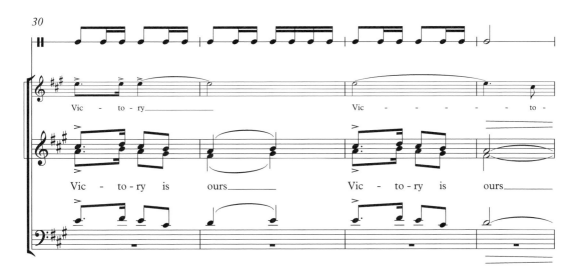

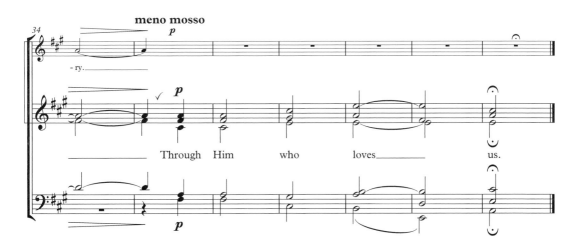

Commissioned by Chris, Mary, Gregory and Jonathan Chivers
for Dominic Chivers on the occasion of his Confirmation,
Pentecost Sunday, 31 May 2009, Blackburn Cathedral
and for performance by Blackburn Cathedral Choir directed by Richard Tanner

A Prayer from South Africa

A Prayer of Alan Paton
(1903–1988)

James Whitbourn

mo-ney, time, pos-ses - sions. Make me__ rea-dy to give ev-en my life if it

mo-ney, time, pos-ses - sions. to give ev-en my life if it

mo-ney, time, pos-ses - sions.

mo-ney, time, pos-ses - sions.

is re-quired of me. And while I have it, use it as an in-stru-ment of your peace,__

is re - quired__ of me. use it as an in-stru-ment of your peace,

use it as an in-stru-ment of your peace,

use it as an in-stru-ment of your peace,

Commissioned by Rochester Cathedral for Christmas Eve 2004
to mark the 1400th anniversary of the cathedral's foundation

A Christmas Gloria

from Missa Carolae

James Whitbourn

tens, om-ni-po-tens, De-us Pa - ter om-ni - po - tens.

tens, om-ni-po-tens.

tens, om-ni-po-tens, De-us Pa - ter om-ni - po - tens.

tens, om-ni-po-tens, De-us Pa - ter om-ni - po - tens.

rit.   5 Meno mosso (= c.104)

Do-mi-ne Fi - li u - ni-ge-ni-te,

Meno mosso (= c.104)

rit.   Solo

Je - su Chri - ste. Do-mi-ne De-us, Ag-nus De - i, Fi - li-us Pa - tris. Qui

tol - lis pec-ca - ta mun - di, mi - se - re - re no - bis. Qui

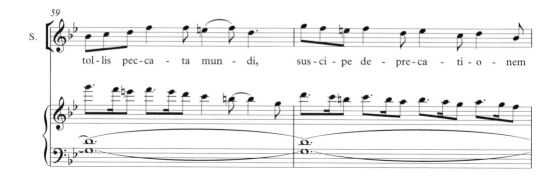

tol - lis pec-ca - ta mun - di, sus-ci - pe de - pre-ca - ti - o - nem

nos - tram. Qui se-des ad dex-te-ram Pa - tris, mi - se - re - re

* small notes for rehearsal only

A great and mighty wonder

St Germanus, trans. J. M. Neale
(1818-1866)

Michael Praetorius (1571-1621)
arr. James Whitbourn

che - ru - bim sing an - thems To shep-herds from___ the sky. Re - peat the hymn a-

che - ru - bim sing an - thems To shep-herds from the sky. Re - peat the hymn a-

Re - peat the hymn a-

Re - peat the hymn a-

-gain! 'To God on high be glo - ry, And peace on earth to men!'

-gain!___ 'To God on high be glo - ry, And peace on___ earth_ to men!'

-gain! 'To God on high be glo - ry, And peace on earth to men!'

-gain! 'To God on high be glo - ry, And peace on earth to men!'

Re - peat the hymn a - gain! 'To God on high be glo - ry, And

Re - peat the hymn a - gain! 'To God on high be glo - ry, And

hands. Re - peat the hymn a - gain! 'To God on high be glo - ry, And

hands. Re - peat the hymn a - gain! 'To God on high be glo - ry, And

peace on earth to men!' 4. Since all he comes to

peace on earth to men!' 4. Since all he comes to

peace on earth to men!' 4. Since all he comes to

peace on earth to men!' 4. Since all he comes to

For Penna A. Rose and the Princeton University Chapel Choir

A Prayer of Cardinal Newman

John Henry Newman (1801–1890)

James Whitbourn

32

Composed for the B.B.C. broadcast coverage of the funeral of
Her Majesty Queen Elizabeth the Queen Mother, April 2002.

Eternal rest

James Whitbourn

Give us the wings of faith

Isaac Watts (1674-1748)

James Whitbourn

*Breathing should, when possible, be staggered in order to maintain the line.

rit.
Tempo primo
13
mf
mp
mp unis.
be. Give us the wings of faith to rise With-in the
bright their glo - ries be Give us wings to
Give us wings to
Give us wings to
cresc.
19
accel.
veil, and see The saints a - bove, how great their joys, How
rise see The saints, How
rise see The saints a - bove, How
rise see The saints a - bove How

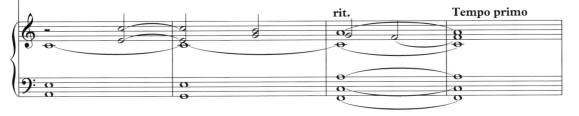

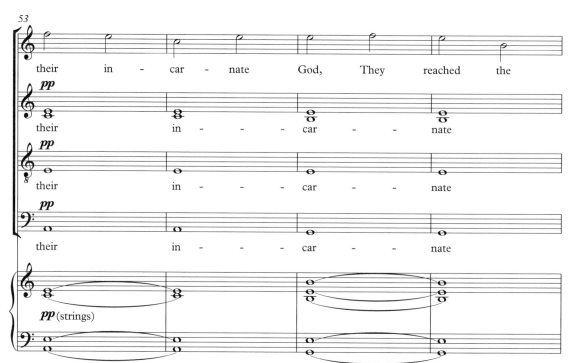

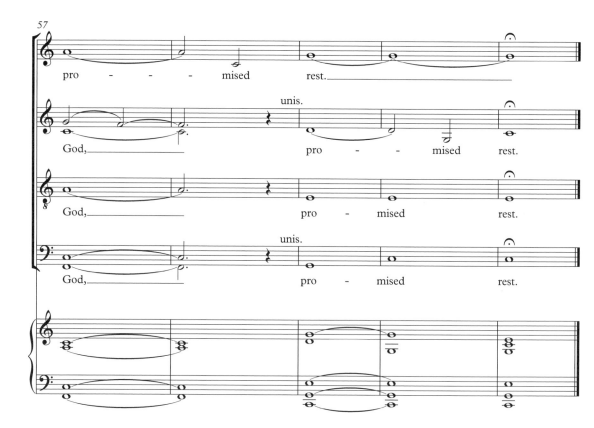

for Stephen Cleobury, Robert Tear and the Choir of King's College, Cambridge
to S. J. W.

Nunc dimittis
from 'Collegium regale' Canticles

James Whitbourn

Liber usualis and
Book of Common Prayer

48

* optional tam-tam part.

50

+ 32' reed

now, and e - ver shall be: world with - out end, A - men, a -

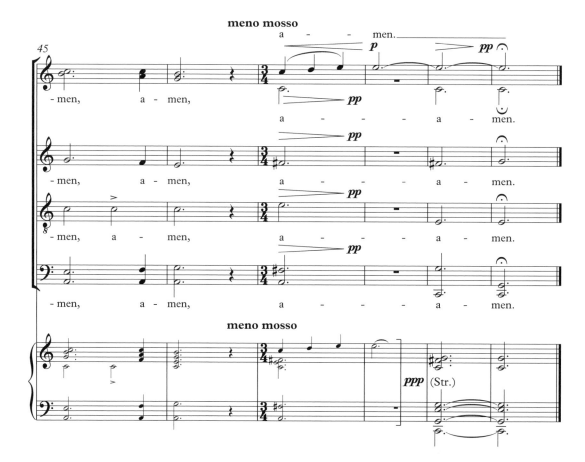

- men, a - men, a - men. a - men.

Commissioned by Dr Joseph Ohrt
and the Choir of Central Bucks High School-West, Doylestown, PA

Pure River of Water of Life

Revelation 22:1-2, 5

James Whitbourn

* these triplet passages a little broader than the main tempo

leaves of the tree were for the heal - ing of the na - tions._____

leaves of the tree were for the heal - ing of the na - tions.

leaves of the tree were for the heal - ing of the na - tions.

leaves of the tree were for the heal - ing of the na - tions.

_____ There shall be no night there, and they_ need no

Wa-ter of life, wa-ter of life, no night there, and they_ need no

Ri - ver, flow - ing, no night there, and they_ need no

Pure ri - ver, no night there, and they_ need no

56

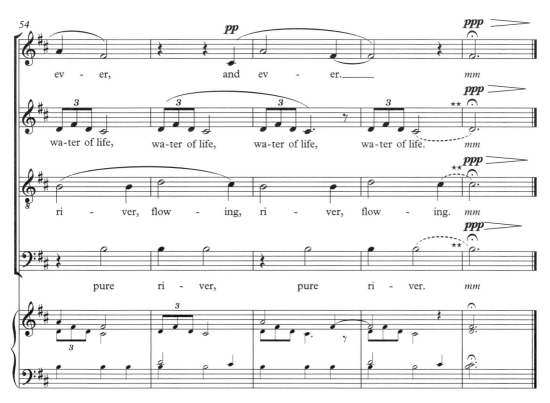

** change to closed lips without a break

To the memory of all cherished friends and loved companions,
especially those who died on September 11th, 2001,
and to the memory of my friend Robert Tear

Lux aeterna
from Requiem canticorum

James Whitbourn

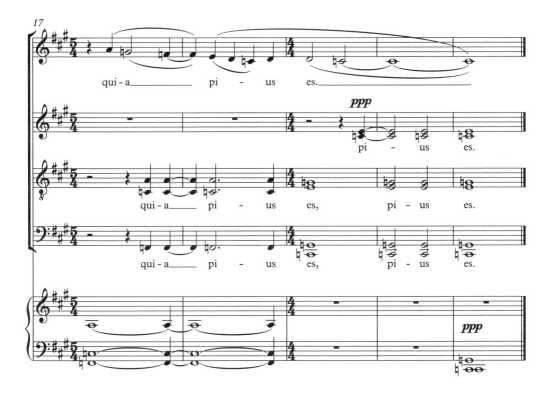

Commissioned by St Wulfram's Church, Grantham with funds from the Philip Lank Trust and the family of John Lodge. First performed 18 December 2011, conducted by Tim Williams.

The Magi's Dream

Robert Tear (1939-2011) James Whitbourn

* to be played by the left hand across two manuals, if the specification of the organ allows it..

Night has come to Be - thle-hem, The

Night has come to Be - thle-hem, The

The

heads are___ filled with a dream-drenched ho - ly ray.___

'Do not re - turn to___ Her - od the king, Go___ back an - oth - er way.'

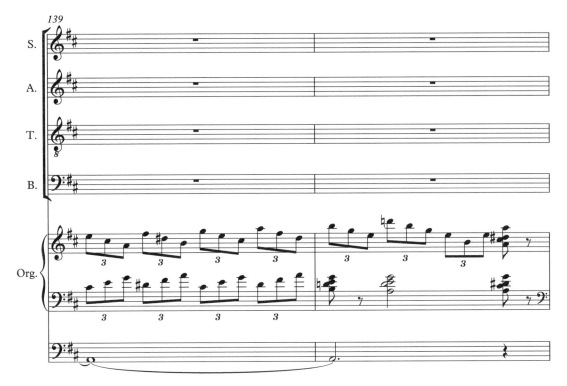

Sa - tan's le -gions, Sa - tan's le -gions, Sa - tan's le -gions to beat.

There is no speech or language

from 'Annelies'

Psalm 19: 3-4
Psalm 79: 3
Lamentations 2: 21

James Whitbourn

none, none who__ could bu - ry them.__ There is no speech or lan-guage

none, none who__ could bu - ry them.__ There is no speech or lan-guage

none, none who__ could bu - ry them.__ There is no speech or lan-guage

none, none who__ could bu - ry them.__ There is no speech or lan-guage

where their voice is____ not heard. The young and the old lie__

where their voice is____ not heard. The young and the old lie__

where their voice is____ not heard. The young and the old lie__

where their voice is____ not heard. The young and the old lie__

on the ground; the maids and young men___ are fall - en.___

on the ground; the maids and young men___ are fall - en.___

on the ground; the maids and young men___ are fall - en.___

___ on the ground; the maids and young men___ are fall - en.___

Meno mosso (♩ = 70)

___ There is no speech or lan-guage where their voice, their voice___ is___ not___ heard.

___ There is no speech or lan-guage where their voice, their voice is not heard.___

___ There is no speech or lan-guage where their voice, their voice is not heard.

___ There is no speech or lan-guage where their voice, their voice is not heard.

Commissioned for the singers of Medina High School, Ohio, Tyler L. Skidmore, conductor, to mark their tour to England and their visit to St Stephen's House, Oxford

Video caelos apertos

Acts 7: 56
Revelation 19: 4 & 4: 11

James Whitbourn

Al - le-lu - ia, A - men, A - men,

lu - ia, A - men, A - men, A -

lu - ia. Al - le-lu - ia, Al - le - lu - ia,

lu - ia. A - men, A - men,___

A - - - men, A - - - men, A -

A - - - men, A - - - men, Al - le -

men, A - - men,___ Al - le - lu - ia, Al - le -

Al - le-lu - ia, Al - - le - lu - ia, Al - le-

___ A - men, Al - le - lu - ia, Al - le -

For Stephen Cleobury and the Choir of King's College Cambridge
to Miranda

Were you there?

American Spiritual
arr. James Whitbourn

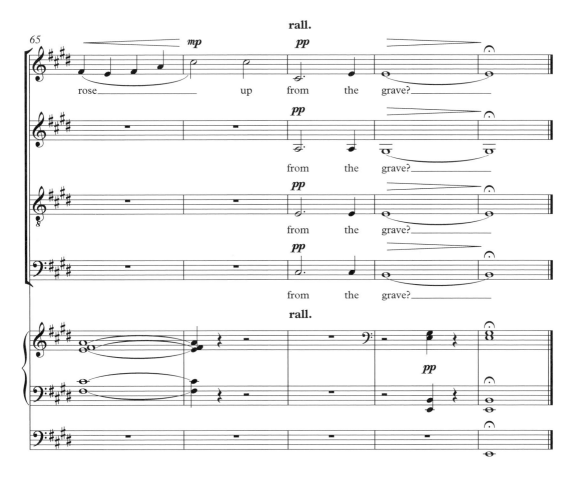

To Alison

Winter's Wait

Robert Tear (1939-2011)

James Whitbourn

8' stopped diapason